"Children and a[...]wering books. The 'Learning to Get Along' series is a powerful tool f[...] [es]sential social skills such as empathy, respect, cooperation, and kindness. This stra[ightforward] [thou]ghtful series helps children visualize how their appropriate behavior positively impacts themselves and others. I heartily recommend this as a solid, classic resource for teaching affective skills to young children."

—**Dr. Stephen R. Covey, Author,** *The 7 Habits of Highly Effective People*

Learning
to Get
Along®

P9-CSE-968

Know and
Follow Rules

Cheri J. Meiners, M.Ed.
Illustrated by Meredith Johnson

free spirit
PUBLiSHiNG®

Helping kids
help themselves™
since 1983

Library of Congress Cataloging-in-Publication Data
Meiners, Cheri J., 1957-
  Know and follow rules : learning to get along / Cheri J. Meiners ; illustrated by Meredith Johnson.
    p. cm.
  ISBN 1-57542-130-5 (alk. paper)
  1. School children--Conduct of life. 2. Obedience--Juvenile literature.
I. Johnson, Meredith ill. II. Title. III. Series: Meiners, Cheri J., 1957– . Learning to get along.
  BJ1631.M39 2005
  646.7'008—dc22

                                                                          2005000172

Cover and interior design by Marieka Heinlen
Edited by Marjorie Lisovskis

10 9 8 7 6 5 4 3 2 1
Printed in Hong Kong

Free Spirit Publishing Inc.
217 Fifth Avenue North, Suite 200
Minneapolis, MN 55401-1299
(612) 338-2068
help4kids@freespirit.com
www.freespirit.com

Dedication

To Kara, who has found
that following rules brings
a clear conscience
and freedom

Acknowledgments

I wish to thank Meredith Johnson, whose charming illustrations resonate so well with the text, and Marieka Heinlen for the exuberant design. I appreciate Judy Galbraith and the entire Free Spirit family for their dedicated support of the series. I am especially grateful to Margie Lisovskis for her diplomatic style as well as her talented editing. I also recognize Mary Jane Weiss, Ph.D., for her expertise and gift in teaching social skills. Lastly, I thank my fantastic family—David, Kara, Erika, James, Daniel, Julia, and Andrea—who are each an inspiration to me.

I go to school with my friends.
We have rules to help us know what to do.

We have rules for play . . .

. . . and we have rules for work.

Sometimes we work quietly.

At other times we speak up.

Rules help us learn.

One rule I know is to listen.
I look at the person talking
and think about what is said.

If I want help, I can ask.

I can follow directions, too.

I do things the first time I am told.

I also do my best.

I think carefully about my work.

I take time to do it well.

Rules help me show respect.

I keep my hands and feet to myself.

I won't use them to bother or hurt anyone.

And I ask permission to use things that aren't mine.

Rules remind me to be polite.

I say "Please," "Thank you,"
and "Excuse me."

I speak kind words in a friendly voice.

I do things to help someone else.

Rules help make things fair for everyone.

When I play games, I follow rules.

I wait my turn.

I let everyone use things.

If there's a problem,
I listen and talk about it,
or get help from a grown-up.

Rules help keep everyone safe, too.

I walk in the hallway.

I also use things carefully.

Each place I go has its own rules.

When I know and follow rules,
things usually work out well.

When I follow rules by myself,
I'm being responsible.

I'm learning and staying safe.

I'm showing respect.

When we all know and follow rules,
it helps us get along!

Ways to Reinforce the Ideas in *Know and Follow Rules*

Know and Follow Rules addresses three important ways rules benefit, strengthen, and support children: *mentally,* by providing clear expectations in the learning environment; *physically,* by helping them stay safe; and *socially,* by helping them to show respect, promote fairness, and get along with others. Because rules differ from setting to setting, few specific rules are delineated in the children's text. Rather, four major objectives are highlighted. Below are the objectives along with possible rules that relate to each. You may want to prepare a poster of the rules for your classroom or learning area. While reading and discussing the book, relate the scenes and rules depicted to your own setting.

Objectives	Possible Rules
Be ready to learn	Listen, follow directions, do your best
Show respect	Keep hands and feet to yourself, ask permission, put materials away, be polite
Get along, be fair	Take turns, share materials, follow game rules
Stay safe	Use things carefully, take care of things, walk indoors

As you read each page spread, ask children:

- What's happening in this picture?
- What rules do you think the people are (person is) remembering?

Here are additional questions you might discuss:

Pages 1–7

- Why do we need rules at school? What might happen if we didn't have rules at school?
- What are some rules that can help you when you play? when you do quiet work? at other times?

Pages 8–13

- What are some rules that can help you learn and do your best?
- Who can you ask if you don't know the rules? (*Make sure children know which adults can help them know and understand rules and when other children might be of help as well.*)

Pages 14–19

- What is respect? (*You might explain respect by saying, "When you show respect to people, you show that you think they are important."*) How does following rules help us show respect?
- What are some rules that help us show respect?
- What does it mean to keep your hands and feet to yourself? (*As necessary, discuss antisocial and dangerous behavior such as hitting, pinching, pushing, and kicking as well as touching and taking people's things.*)
- What does it mean to ask permission? When do you ask permission at school? What should you do if the person says yes? What if the person says no?
- How does being polite show respect? How do you feel when someone is polite to you? When someone *isn't* polite? What other friendly words can you use to show respect? What are some polite things you can do for other people?

Pages 20–23

- Why do games have rules? What might happen if people tried to play games without any rules at all?
- How do rules make games fair? *(Discuss this in the context of specific games children play in your setting.)*
- Have you ever played a game when you didn't know or follow the rules? When someone else didn't know or follow the rules? What happened?
- If someone isn't following the rules, what can you do?
- Is it okay to change the rules of a game? *(It can still be fair for everyone if all players agree to the rules.)*
- Have you ever made up your own rules for a game? How did it work out?

Pages 24–25

- What are some rules at school that help keep us safe?
- Why is it important to walk instead of run in the hallways and classroom?
- What are some things at school we need to use carefully?

Pages 26–27

- Why do you think we have different rules for different places? *(Discuss different rules you have in various situations and places in your setting, such as in the block area, housekeeping center, art area; on the playground or bus; in the cafeteria, halls, bathrooms; during quiet work time, games, playtime; and so forth.)*
- What are some rules that you know and follow at home? in other places?
- What is a rule that we follow everywhere? Why is it always important? What's another rule we follow everywhere? *(Focus here on rules that ensure that everyone is safe and treated with respect.)*
- If you could make your own rules (for your own room, or for an imaginary place) what would they be? Why would you want those rules? How would they help everyone who came there?

Pages 28–31

- What does it mean to be responsible? *(You might explain this by saying, "When you're responsible, you do what you know is right.")* How does following rules show that you are responsible?
- How does being responsible help keep you safe?
- Can you help someone else know and follow rules? How?
- How do rules help us get along?

"Following Rules" Games

Read this book often with your child or group of children. Once children are familiar with the book, refer to it when teachable moments arise involving the need to know, understand, and follow rules. Make it a point to notice and comment when children follow rules that help them show respect, play fair, stay safe, and get ready to learn. In addition, use the following activities to reinforce children's understanding of rules and why we need them.

What's the Rule?

Preparation: If you haven't done so already, make a poster of your classroom rules (see page 32) and discuss the rules with children. On index cards, write individual scenarios similar to the following. Place the cards in a bag.

Sample Rules:

1. **Listen and follow directions**
2. **Share and take turns**
3. **Hands and feet to yourself**
4. **Put things away**

Sample Scenarios:

- Matt walked quietly down the hall with his hands at his side.
- After Shayna built a house out of Legos, she took it apart and put the Lego bin back on the shelf.
- Madeleine waited to climb the slide until the person at the top slid and moved away.
- Danny grabbed a toy from another boy.
- As the teacher talked, Elise was looking at the goldfish.
- After Kaitlyn sorted buttons at the math center, she left them on the table.
- Samir got the crayons out of his desk when his teacher asked.
- Jordan liked Kerry's braids so much that he pulled on them gently when she sat near him.

Level 1

Have a child draw a card. Read or have a child read it aloud. Ask, "Is the child following one of our rules?" Then ask, "What rule is the child following?" or, "Which rule should the child remember?" Continue having children draw cards and discuss rules.

Level 2

After each card has been drawn and read, do one of the following: If the scenario describes children following rules, have one or two children act out the scene. Ask the other children the questions in Level 1. If a child in the scenario has forgotten to follow a rule, discuss the rule (or rules) that should be applied. Then have children role-play the scenario, enacting an appropriate solution.

Reasons for Rules

Preparation: On four large sheets of drawing paper, write the following headings and add simple drawings: "Be Ready to Learn" (book), "Show Respect" (two heads smiling at one another), "Get Along" (two stick figures holding hands), and "Stay Safe" (stop sign). Mount the four sheets on the bulletin board or a large whiteboard. Write each of your class rules on an index card, or select rules from the list on page 32. Place the cards in a bag. Have additional index cards on hand.

Directions: Ask a child to draw a card. Read or have a child read the rule on the card aloud. Ask questions like the following: "Why do we have this rule?" "What does this rule help us do?" "What might happen if we didn't follow this rule?" During the discussion, have children decide which heading (reason) the rule should go under. Then, the child who picked the card can tape or pin it under the appropriate heading. Some rules are important for more than one reason; for example, taking turns on a slide fits under "Stay Safe" and also "Get Along." Talk about how a single rule can help in more than one way. (If you wish, write the rule on more than one index card and mount it under all appropriate headings.) Encourage children to think of several situations, in and out of the classroom, where rules are needed for one or more reasons.

Rule Riddles

Follow the preparation for "Reasons for Rules," on page 34. Select a card and give clues about the rule. For example, for "Listen" you might say, "I'm thinking of a rule that helps us learn. It helps us know what someone said." You might also give examples such as, "Ally heard the teacher say 'Line up.'" Have children guess the rule to solve the riddle. A child can then put the card under an appropriate heading.

Knowing Rules in Many Places

Preparation: Cut out pictures from magazines that show nonschool settings where rules are important, such as a store, street, swimming area, and kitchen. Glue the pictures to large pieces of card stock. Think of one to three rules for each setting; write each rule on an index card. Stack the cards of rules facedown on a table.

Directions: Point to each pictured setting and ask, "What place is this? What do people do here?" Then have or help a child pick and read a card with a rule. Ask, "Where would this rule be important?" For example, "Look both ways before you walk" would be important when crossing a street. After an appropriate setting is chosen, let the child place the rule card near that picture.

Extension: Discuss the reasons for some of the rules, using questions like these: "Why do you think we don't handle breakable things at the store?" "What might happen if you went in the pool without a buddy?"

Variation: Invite children to role-play ways to follow the rules discussed.

Our Class Rules! Signs

Materials: Construction paper, scissors, crayons or markers, Popsicle sticks, tape

Directions: Discuss how traffic signs show the rules for driving. Have children make their own signs based on the rules in your classroom. Have children cut construction paper into various shapes and sizes and write a class rule on their sign. When finished, have or help them tape a Popsicle stick to the back of the sign.

Extension: Using the scenarios from the "What's the Rule?" game on page 34 (or others of your own), read an index card and have children hold up their signs when they apply.

Variations: Have children create a poster by mounting their signs on another piece of paper with the title "Our Class Rules!" Decorate the poster with illustrations for each rule. Or compile an "Our Class Rules!" book by having children create pictures of ways to follow rules. Each rule on a sign can mark the beginning of a chapter. Use construction paper or cardstock to make the book's cover, and a hole punch and yarn to bind the book.

"My Imaginary Rules" Drawing

Discuss what rules the children think are important, and what might happen if there were no rules. Then have children think of an imaginary place, such as a castle or an island, and the rules they would want in it. Have the children draw a picture of themselves in that place. Assist them in writing one to three rules. Discuss why they chose those rules and whether the rules would be good for everyone.

Other titles in Free Spirit's Learning to Get Along® series:

Our Learning to Get Along series by Cheri J. Meiners, M.Ed., helps children learn, understand, and practice basic social and emotional skills. Real-life situations, lots of diversity, and concrete examples make these read-aloud books appropriate for childcare settings, schools, and the home. Each book focuses on a specific skill and ends with ideas for reinforcing what the children have learned. Each book: $10.95, 40 pp., color illust., S/C, 9" x 9", ages 4–8.

TALK AND WORK IT OUT
Peaceful conflict resolution is simplified so children can learn to calm down, state the problem, listen, and think of and try solutions.

RESPECT AND TAKE CARE OF THINGS
Encourages children to put things back where they belong and ask permission to use things that don't belong to them. Teaches simple environmental awareness.

TRY AND STICK WITH IT
Introduces children to flexibilty, stick-to-it-iveness (perserverance), and the benefits of trying something new.

LISTEN AND LEARN
Introduces and explains what listening means, why it's important to listen, and how to listen well.

UNDERSTAND AND CARE
Builds empathy in children; guides them to show they care by listening to others and respecting their feelings.

SHARE AND TAKE TURNS
Gives reasons to share; describes four ways to share; points out that children can also share their knowledge, creativity, and time.

JOIN IN AND PLAY
Teaches the basics of cooperation, getting along, making friends, and being a friend.

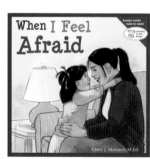

WHEN I FEEL AFRAID
Helps children understand their fears; teaches simple coping skills; encourages children to talk with trusted adults about their fears.

BE POLITE AND KIND
Introduces children to good manners and gracious behavior including saying "Please," "Thank you," "Excuse me," and "I'm sorry."

To place an order or to request a free catalog of SELF-HELP FOR KIDS®
and SELF-HELP FOR TEENS® materials, please write, call, email, or visit our Web site:

Free Spirit Publishing Inc.
217 Fifth Avenue North • Suite 200 • Minneapolis, MN 55401 • toll-free 800.735.7323 • local 612.338.2068
fax 612.337.5050 • help4kids@freespirit.com • www.freespirit.com